VOLUME I

Flowers of Love

To Chris Claucter from members of Vietnamese Amateur Poets Society. Tina Hellan

Vietnamese Amateur Poets Society

1998

VOLUME I

Flowers Of Love

Vietnamese Amateur Poets Society
P.O Box 246958
Sacramento, CA 95824 - USA
Tel/Fax: (916) 391-5277

Acknowledgements

The Vietnamese Amateur Poets Society gratefully acknowledges the contributions of the following people in the organization of the First International Poetry Convention in Sacramento in 1998 to commemorate the 4th anniversary of the founding of the Society in 1994. The publication of this first volume of collections of poems, entitled "Flowers of Love" is a testimony to their efforts and marks the growth of the Society into an international forum for artistic development.

- David Tam Ha, M.D
- Phung Vo Ha, M.D
- Mr. Do Thien Thinh
- Mr. Daivd Du Tran
- Mr. Ba Van Le & Assn.
- Mr. Hien Huu Nguyen
- Mr. Trac Pham
- Mr. Buu Duc Duong
- Mr. Nhuan Xuan Le
- Mr. Nghia Pham

Sacramento, September 1998
The Vietnamese Amateur Poets Society

FOREWORD

Founded in the Fall of 1994 by a group of Vietnamese expatriate poets, the Vietnamese Amateur Poets Society (VAPS) began its annual publication of collections of Vietnamese Poems, entitled "Flowers of Love", in early 1995. So far, four volumes of Vietnamese poetry have been published. The Society's goals are to enrich Vietnamese cultural heritage abroad and to preserve Vietnamese language for younger generations through the medium of poetry.

In conjunction with an International Poetry convention held in Sacramento from September 11 through 13, 1998 to commemorate the 4th anniversary of its founding, VAPS is publishing this English version of the Vietnamese "Flowers of Love" compendium to introduce Vietnamese poetry to English speakers worldwide.

It is our fervent hope that this collection of poems will be enthusiastically received by lovers of poetry everywhere, to help promote intercultural understanding between Vietnamese and Americans as well other ethnic groups, especially Asians, throughout the world.

The Vietnamese Amateur Poets Society

Flowers of Love

Poems Collection

cover design:
Huynh Ngoc Diep

art direction:
Ha Anh Tu

picture by:
Vuong Thu Thuy - Paris

typesetting:
Nguyen Ham

presented by:
Vietnamese Amateur Poets Society - USA

Flowers of Love

Authors:

NHU HOA LE QUANG SINH - NGUYEN PHUC SONG HUONG - THU VAN - LE SY DONG - PHAM NHA DU - NGUYEN THI SEN TRANG - CAO MY NHAN - PHAM NGOC - PHAM TRUNG THANH - LE NGUYEN - VU DUC TO CHAU - NGOC AN - TRONG KHANH - NGUYEN PHUONG - HO MONG THIEP - TYNA - DO HUU - VU HOI - NGUYEN PHAN NHAT NAM - HUONG NAM - LE TRONG NGHIA - TRAC PHAM - PAUL CAO - KIM PHUONG TRAN - LE VAN BA - THU MINH - TRAN TINH NHU - NGUYEN NGUYEN THANH - PHAM THUONG HOP - LUU TRAN NGUYEN - DIEN LINH LE KHAC LY - TINA THANH HUONG - DIEM THY - NAM GIAO - HUYNH NGOC DIEP - N.T. KHANH MINH - NGUYEN DUC CUONG - NGUYEN THUY LINH - NGUYEN VAN CUONG - THANH THANH

Nhu Hoa Le Quang Sinh

TWIN STARS
(GEMINI)

We both, two bright stars
Ever and ever go deep and far
And hang freely in the sky
We conserve our love of twin stars.

Hand in hand, we, together
Cast our eyes further and further
To the warm horizon of hope
And go forward, we, together,

We are care-free from bustle
Despite great changes to the world
Our love is everlasting and firm
Reachable of life's bliss, why disturb?

Our universe is so immense
And our world goes high and far
Among points of lights and planets
We, forever, twin stars.

Nhu Hoa Le Quang Sinh

Up higher and higher
We look at each other
Disregarding obscurity ahead
Our eyes grow brighter.

When you turn to your twenties
My future has just passed
Born on the lucky day of birth
We are both souls of mirth.

Nhu Hoa Le Quang Sinh

FAREWELL MONTEREY

Spring in Monterey
At the end of Fremont Street
Stretching out to the sea,
I met her.
She looked into my eyes
With eyes of deep blue
As blue as the Ocean.

She asked, When was VN founded?
I answered, My country is as old as my age,
Four thousand years of civilization
With such heroes as sisters TRUNG, TRIEU,
And TRAN HUNG DAO, QUANG TRUNG
And everlasting war in this era.

I asked, How about America?
She answered,
My country is as young as my age,
Two hundred years since it was founded,
It has had wars and heroes
But yields nothing in this era
Except for ARMSTRONG.

Nhu Hoa Le Quang Sinh

Summer in Monterey
I said good-bye to her
At the end of Fremont Street
Stretching out to sea.
She asked, When the war will end?
I answered, Can't tell the future!
I asked, When our love will end?
She looked into my eyes
With eyes of deep blue
Did not say...

4/4/74 Monterey, CA

Nhu Hoa Le Quang Sinh

LEAVING THE BASE OF
THE STATUE OF LIBERTY

Under the Statue of Liberty, I feel giddy
With the light erected from the flame of Bastilles
The Goddess of Liberty raises her torch,
Anh its light reflects off the ocean,
spreading over the Earth.
It focuses on the Soviet Union
and severe Eastern Europe,
Passing by Cuba, Viet Nam, China and Korea,
Now the light is growing dim, hidden by black clouds,
And over the sky of Zaire, the light goes out,
As five hundred thousand Tutsis are surrounded
by darkness,
Making Man's conscience plunge into blackness.

Nhu Hoa Le Quang Sinh

From the torch in the hand of the Goddess of Liberty,
The light of freedom shines across Harlem, Manhattan,
and Washington D.C.,
Where the leaders, in the name of freedom,
founded America, a civilized country.
But because of crimes and violence,
the house are locked up all the time.
Thinking of Nghieu, Thuan's time*,
people didn't bother to pick up
dropped objects on the streets,
nor did they need to shut their doors at night.
Nowadays, with Revolution and Freedom,
Mankind is confounded by worry and fear.

Leaving the base of the Statue of Liberty,
as if I were falling from the moon
between reality and dream; between good and evil;
law and justice.
Oh! Liberty! In your name,
Mankind has exterminated the conscience of men.

*Nghiem, Thuan, the kings of old China

Nhu Hoa Le Quang Sinh

A SMILE IN BLOOMS

-To Mrs. Illa Collin

The Sun rises on the azure horizon
On green hill, the morning-dews are shining
As Illa Collin's smile blooms like a rose
To the cool breeze, that is shaking.

Nguyen Phuc Song Huong

SO FAR

The sea the reality
At somewhere very far,
So far but I can see
Someday when I will start.

Your heart the reality
In you but at somewhere
So far, further from me
Someday my love declared

Nguyen Phuc Song Huong

THE WHITE SORROW

Who, the genius painter
Threw color into nature
That the leaves in fall with red,
Brown and yellow in winter.

It just snowed last night
Everywhere now in the whole white,
The mountains,
The rivers,
The forest,
The wings of birds
The backs of deers
And on my lonely shoulders!

The genius painter
Who threw color into nature
Threw sorrow into my heart
The white sorrow...

Nguyen Phuc Song Huong

A KIND OF FLOWER
FOR VIETNAM

(Diamond Homer Prize
Famous Poets Society - Hollywood, CA1995)

Some flower seeds that given were rotten,
Sprouted some, but grown ill-thriven
I asked if my friend want another
" A kind of perennial" They answered
" The one that not sow in the ground,
But nicely open in our torn soul."
I knew which one they have desired;
The immortal all wish to admire.
The miracle that the world blooming
Human life with everlasting springs
News and news from my old homeland.
Come to me with my people's pain,
Must hate still has been pouring down,
How could the flower of truth be grown?

Forgiveness how good you live without!

Thu Van

TO MY COUNTRY

Beloved Country!
Now wrapped in your bosom
My soul feels hurt at the thought of leaving.
Every tree, every blade of grass,
means so much for me,
And, white in the dusk, flocks of birds flying.

Soon in a foreign land, I will be a stranger,
My heart will yearn for you forever.
Huyen Tran's departure has gained 0 and Ly
*provinces,**
In my turn, what will I do not to blush with shame?

Mother, I feel responsibilities weighing,
And my heart grieves over my dear children's
absence.
Let me listen, in the distance,
To the call of reunion and happiness.

Thu Van

Confined, for over half my life,
My hair's faded from countless ups and downs,
A migrant bird, of freedom I long for space,
Before you can await my return,
be courageous to say good-bye.

If crying is feminine weakness,
Let me shed for once
Tears of attachment and faithfulness
To you, country, and my beloved ones!

*Princess Huyen Tran was sent to Champa in 1306 to
politically marry Che Man, King of Champa, who, in return,
offered the 0 & Ly provinces to Vietnam.

Thu Van

THE CONFINED MUSE

From whom does the lake water ondulate ?
In vain, the beautiful weeping willow
Reflects its gracious shape
At the same time splendid and filled with sorrow.

For whom the blue sky, the light breeze,
The full-bloom rose fragrancing the astmosphere,
The church bells voice in the twilight,
The delicious music in the moonlight ?

For whom the all-bathed-in-drew-iris,
The loving butterfly brushing
Against the voluptuous petals, the swan reflecting
In the blue waters her immaculate dress ?

What lost illusions! What betrayed hopes
What blank hours spent sleepily.
The space, mother of birds flying off,
Wastes away: The Muse is confined.

French poem " LA MUSE ENFERMÉE"
English version by the author herself.

Le Sy Dong

OLD NEWS CARRIER

(Diamond Homer Prize
by Famous Poets Society's 95 Contest)

*His Light leads me
On the way I feel free
Already gone three cold winters
In the natural refrigerator.*

*Extremely alone
In the darkness I've gone
For safety I pray him
So strong even dimmed.*

*The scattered yellow leaves
I've been walking on
I've been walking on
The scattered yellow leaves*

*The long streets I passed by
The hot news run in late night
To my dear readers
Before the dawn begins to raise*

*Its coldness and my agingness
I gather feeling and compassion and knowledge
From everyone on the human planet
Through papers GOD'S LOVE exists.*

Le Sy Dong

CALI'S SPRING

Overpasses the two great blue oceans
Under the immense sky
Up and down and only boatman
The roaring's rolling a miserable point
side and side

Forty hard years
" Moses and Moses" promised Land
Ragged black winter with rude nude trees
Into the spring with multi-floral scent
Entered Cali splendid life I see.

Cali's Spring
watch on the green grass everywhere
Yellow and yellow, purple and purple,
red and red, and white and white.
Embellish Cali and flourish country there
Look at onto the grey branches
the blue sprouts open wide

Cali's Spring the sun is warm
The shine dolce in the light yellow
The musical sound anywhere raises charm
Coming here from the hell the paradise I get now.

Pham Nha Du

MOON HILL

Between two sides of death and living
There's a new moon hanging somewhere
On the voyage of human being
There's me wandering here and there.

In the plant, pine hill, wild
Hide sleeping in a doubtful life
Further, long hell who backs wondering about
Asking myself where's understanding idea,
I found

Call intimates but back with strange sound
A life way, dark and blue, and now
Dwelling in a coma, deep and fear
Beyond the living, happiness appears ?

Still mild and innocent forever, the moon
Shining throughout lives down and full
Will know, who knows who no way
I have found myself for long, long days.

Dalat, 1990

Cao My Nhan

A MELODY

It was always you with your air pensively deep,
Your stride with hesitation on the hill steep,
Your image glimmering through cigarette smoke,
Night after night pity for my heart to evoke;
Always you and myself sitting one another by
And watching the shooting stars in the high sky.
It was always you, honey, with that bright smile
And myself till the war-end waiting all the while.
Let me bring you into our dear wonders' land
For you forever to sing songs of sweet brand
Lulling me into my long nostalgic night-time:
Beside tired weapons thousand of a love rhyme.

Vietnamese poem" Khúc Du Ca"
English version by THANH THANH

Nguyen Thi Sen Trang

COME TO ME
AND STAY FOREVER

Come to me and stay forever.
Let your heart be calm in the setting sun.
Get the peace for which you've been longing
After years of struggling.

Come to me and stay forever.
Let go off grief and worries.
Be gleeful and let your heart thrill,
When love songs melodiously start murmuring

Come to me and stay forever.
No need to look any further.
For here you find a warm and loving heart,
To help melt away your anguish and exile.

Nguyen Thi Sen Trang

DEW DROP
OR TEAR DROP?

By the edge of a ridge,
Currents of water swirl below.
At Santa Cruz beach,
On an early autumn day.

I lose my calm and
Fall into his arms.
Oh love is so fierce!
And a long winding road ahead.

Flowers of love blossom up
Everywhere so romantically.
1, like a worker bee,
Am lost with sweet honey.

Forest full of wonderful fragrance,
Sky full of stars and moon,
1, like a small swallow,
Not knowing her way back.

Nguyen Thi Sen Trang

Soon comes September.
Clouds gather into walls.
Gone with the dreams,
Love is like sparkling dew.

Dew drop or tear drop?
There's still so much of life.
I, alone in the sea of love.
Surrounded by waves of passion.

Dreams of life flourishing,
Wild remains my heart.
Oh, love is so fierce,
And a long winding road ahead!

Nguyen Thi Sen Trang

"CHOPIN BY THE SEA"

Come wash the shore,
Cleansing waves of the winter sea.
Wash away trouble and worry.
Leave me with bliss and peace,
Brighten the dark world with glistening foam
Gleeful to greet the coming season.
Warm the hearts of lonely souls,
Splash happiness to the miserable,
Fill the air with the bright light
Of glorious spray!

I want to hear the pure sweet song of love
And listen to the hopeful symphony
Of Chopin by the sea.
Come to the shore,
Wandering waves of the winter sea.
Bring back the missing fisherman,
To revive the joy of their children
Send back the long lost sailors,
To cheer the faces of their widows.

All the world waits to celebrate that special moment.
To toast the joy so reborn,
While the sky still resounds the wonderful melodies
Of Chopin by the sea.

(Inspired by the symphony "Chopin by the Sea" played by P.Banak)

Nguyen Thi Sen Trang

AWAKENNING CONSCIOUSNESS

When a rose perishes in the intense heat,
The Sun is in a rage,
Trying to burn all the Earth's sprouts of birth and
death.
O! the ignorant swirling fire!
You are so insane with your wrath.
The whole world will be burnt to ash
With your furious cyclone.
I pray for the revival of human compassion.
Searching for the tranquility of the deep subconscious,
Where the magnificent beauty, brightened by the
celestial light,
More exalted and loftier than any glory,
Governs the highest wisdom of mankind.
The awakening of inner consciousness will strongly
incite human nature,
Affect the supreme mentality,
Increase benevolence and generosity,
Lessen human suffering and agony
Destroy hatred and envy.
When an inner wisdom pervades the universe.
The flowers of happiness blossom
With the fragrance of sandalwood permeating the air.
The celestial music fills the entire world.
From the deepest consciousness,
Beams of love flood every corner of the universe.

Flowers of Love - 33

Pham Ngoc

"GOODBYE" CANNOT BE A WORD OF EXPRESSION

The last time we met
there was nothing left to say
the echoes of your sobbing
filled the air
the sorrows in me
vast as the night sky
the final word was silenced
because "goodbye" cannot be a word of expression
All of the memories that we shared
rushing back within me
like fractures on an empty field
after the quake

Snow has started to fall
covering the deserted street
the sign of winter is coming
and the last rainy day just disappearing
the only thing left now
is the air filled with the blameless white snow
from afar
a lost bird
crashed into the mountain slope
subsiding

Pham Ngoc

I have been hoping for a slight shade of sunlight
I have been looking into an empty crater
for obsessions that no longer remained
You have been transformed
into the everlasting flower
that is forever within me
The pains and sorrows that I have endured
will never end
This strenuous and troubled life
is just like a boat in a stormy sea
that has never seen a peaceful day
Love and happiness that I have been searching for
is just a dream that continues to glitter
but will never near

And finally
everything is just an illusion
Dream and reality
continuing to embrace each other
You and I
heading in different directions
Dreams still hovering around
reality has become tears
that are crumbling down...

THE BEGINNING OF DESIRE

Finally -
we are apart
you have returned to your strenuous life
the heated passion of younger time
buried deep in my mind
I am moving on
carrying with me fresh pain
and faded memories
The wicked smile
and sweet sound of your voice
still echo
like the howling of the spirits at night

Love -
is the express train that never stops
the lost traveler staring through the corner
of deepest sky
searching for any sign of what remains
from the train that just passed by
Night will fall
and the murky cloud will surround
this wasted land
where he is stranded

Pham Ngoc

Happiness -
is a delicate flower in the wind
one day
it will be blown away
And in desperation
I am continuing to search
with obstacles around me
for the vision of life
time passing by, the pains remain alive
Like a free bird
In the immense sky
nowhere to turn
the jungle is filled with unseen traps
and dangers envelop its flight

Finally -
in shattered love
even a stone will agonize
like thousand pieces of broken glass
still reflect the segregation and suffering
and in deep remembrances
we will return to
the beginning of desire

Pham Ngoc

IT SEEMS THAT ...
THE STORM FROM HUE (1)
HAS JUST PASSED BY HERE

El Nîno

The big storm has just passed by
The wind blows in the East
The rain floods the Western fields
From Salt Lake City
to Hayward hills.

* * *

It seems that
someone's just given up the carefree life
and in me
the smile has just faded away
When the storm goes through Hue (1)
there are boats sunk during the dark night.

The roads leading to Central Hue
Soak wet after the rain
The monsoon season is rushing in
and take away all the autumn leaves.

Pham Ngoc

It seems that
there is a flower fallen in the late night
When the storm passes by
The sound of life
filled with sorrows and pains.

It seems that
There is a lotus light
flickering on the Huong River (2) one night
that has just faded away
The fresh memories still linger
in the heart of a traveler
Once listening to the wicked sound of music
of a singer in the boat gliding on the river
And tears are hiding deep in the sadness of her eyes
It seems that
the boat has just left for the high seas.

From a far away place
The storm has just passed by here
It seems that
in my heart
sadness just comes near...

(1)Hue, a city in central Vietnam
(2)Huong River that runs through the city of Hue

Nude   *Vuong Thu Thuy - PARIS*

Pham Trung Thanh

SUNSHINE IN THE HONGKONG FORBIDDEN CAMP

The sunshine is cavorting around, in its play
With wind and clouds: what freedom composition!
I feast my eyes upon each innocent beam, ray,
Like a round eye wide open on the leafy partition.

Oh, how much I cherish that summer sunshine?
As I am quite a lot fond of the leaves on the trees;
I also love the sweet wind and to see it run fine
Like the white clouds softly floating in the breeze.

But the HongKong sunshine, to me, is not nice
Especially to all of boatpeople here these crowds.
Poor sunshine! It cannot get of the cake any slice;
Locked in, with us, it enjoys no wind and clouds.

I catch to fondle in each caring though little hand
Each jot of sunshine, like me, the fences cramp.
To await a tomorrow, I will together with it stand,
To take dear sunshine out of this forbidden camp.

Vietnamese poem "*Nắng Trong Trại Cấm Hồng Kông*"
English version by THANH THANH

Flowers of Love - 41

Le Nguyen

BACK IN THE OLD TOWN

Back in the old town
With sadness surrounding
Autumn sun fading from the sky
Memories of the time has gone by
The road that we once shared
Now divided
It has weathered murky cloud,
Hot humid sun, monsoon rain
Sorrow and pain
The bridge over the Huong(1) River
And the city of Hue(2)
shadowed under the monarchy era
My beloved city from afar
Even in hard or joyous time
That autumn cloud
Will always be in my mind

Vietnamese poem *"Về Quê Cũ"*
English version by PHẠM NGỌC

(1) Huong River that runs through the city of Hue
(2) In central Vietnam, Hue was the Imperial Capital

Le Nguyen

DREAM

Oh the wind! Give me the fragrant air
From your lips - the heaven that I dream
The shy moon stares at our love
Ocean waves caress your body
Oh the Sun! Don't fade away in the twilight
On me will it always shine
Even the river has lost its way
Memories of you never sway
In reality, in dream
And thousand miles away
My love for you
Is here to stay

Vietnamese poem *"Vu Vơ"*
English version by PHẠM NGỌC

Vu Duc To Chau

DAY OF RETURN...

Following in woodcutter's footsteps,
I've descended from Mountain
In the evening, over the worn paths,
I've taken a farewell.
In front, the nostalgia evoked me,
the distant recollection
Backwards, the forest of moon was tired of waiting,
on the top of hill.

At that day, on my return, I haven't a mat
The pillar of the inclined house, laid in the night,
beside the sweet grass
I was stupefied to death,
in regarding the moon through the hole of shadow
Every candle has fallen away, lighted again, lack of you.

During many years,
my hair has been whitened and I've done as the wind,
Strolling about the clouds in the sky, singing on, the
mountain.
My friend, living in the "thatched hut",
in the period of "Three Kingdoms",
Was crazy too, beside the "inclined cave",
under the rain.

Vu Duc To Chau

When I've returned, how pitiful was my mother,
being alive, at that day!
By the deep affection, the tears from the bottom,
have inversely overflowed
Over the evening dew, with the smoke in the kitchen,
my old country was blurred
The native land became white
and the vicissitude purple too, in the sky.

At that day, when I've descended,
the river was still running.
The boat, without my lover,
drifted with heaven, on the waves.
From thousand of miles, the country was very far away,
with Tu Ma's love.
The "Song of Ty-Ba guitar" was resounded
from "Tam-Duong ferry-landing".

Full of tears, I've returned, at that day!
In the obscured smoke and dust,
I've gone in the twilight.
Over the footprints on the lands,
I've still missed the moon-lights,
Remaining in my soul, the last feelings of poetry.

Vietnamese poem " Ngày Về "
English version by LƯU HOÀI

Ngoc An

AWAY
FROM THE MURKY SHORE

Why have you come to this world of sins
This sea of life , death and suffering
For survival you have to carry the chain of slavery
For power and influence ,
 you endure a blighted destiny.

I happened to be a silk worm on a murky shore
To pay my due in silk to the world
My frail boat went astrayed unto the bank of passion
And picked up an alga to sail toward the ocean ...

Heading into the immense dust storm
Where earthly people experience pain and sorrow
Where my frail boat faces furious typhoons
Where the sand from the sea bottom
buries my aching heart

Ngoc An

Why did you come here at this unpropitious time
When your life is in bondage
like your knuckled hands ?
How longer will it take you to settle back
and forth your debts
From your forgone destiny
that tortured you to the death ?

A hundred years of blessings on this earthly shelter
Cannot compare
with a thousand happy years in the Nirvana
Please help my boat sail away from the murky shore
My godly lover of the unfathomable infinity .

Vietnamese poem *"Qua Bờ Bến Đục"*
English version by DU PHƯỚC LONG Ph.D

Ngoc An

THE SORROW
OF CERTAIN SPRING

The Spring's coming in this foreign country
My remembrance suddenly aims at a small city
Vung Tau town with its morning sun
and rainy evenings
Where're they now
those beautiful landscapes of springs ?

Oh! My Country, it's too far right now..
I'm missing my father for years in the South
And he probably thinks of us,
those who must be separated
Due to the destiny of our Country
that providing our needs

Plenty of patriotism, my father's now eighty six of age
He's planned to remain there uncountable for
disadvantages
My sibling once got a tearful farewell with the town
Where my father's posture
was migrained in me until now

Ngoc An

So as his recommendations to us at that day
We're realized it for future without delay
Because of our homeland, we spent most of our time
So be better off our knowledge during our lifetime

There're many times , we couldn't go home visiting
So offer him our best wishes for the beginning of Spring
Here you're some of my poetry today
On spite of oceanic distances that separate our way

Please understand us showing our love
toward parents there
That you and your children both sides are distanced by
hemispheres
Your hair, we think, now becomes completely gray
Perhaps you're there crucially distressed
and here we dismay

In the other side from the Pacific Ocean
My mother's eternally resting calm
During seven years with her lonely clay
Oh! mother,
your soul is a breakthrough of our narrow days
We're here from the Ocean of Remembrance
Nobody knows that we're crying over the sea immense

Vietnamese poem "Nhớ Xuân Xưa"
English version by NGÔ ĐA THIỆN

Ngoc An

REVEALING LYRIC

There was once I look like a leaf withering
Facing dreams nights crying over my appearance.
Hearing in the cold penthouse crickets whispering
Arousing dole in their monotonous perseverance.

I then seemed nearly to be kind of alga blades
Drifting along with such an immense water flow
Where was each petal of time falling in the shakes
To make my poor lonely soul so tinted with woe?

I was the image of those dewdrops it appeared,
In the twilight, when the late sun had set deep,
To get broken up on the leaves at once cleared;
I embraced my discontent in every solitary sleep.

I felt myself similar to a willow dried and bare
Standing lonesome by that roadside segregated
Listening to the coming autumn in a breath of air.
No more past halo: for what was it to be waited?

Ngoc An

But now however, all of a sudden, I 've got you.
A lovable love which we both have just fondly lit.
Oh yes, how this passion acts as a ball of fire due
To light my heart with innermost feelings in it.

I had heretofore spent half of my dear existence
And it had left me only the moment of grief rife.
Let me use that remaining half of my subsistence
To share with you the ups and downs of our life.

Vietnamese Poem "*Khúc Tự Tình*"
English version by THANH THANH

Trong Khanh

THE WAR

There are those I've seen today,
Lying face down in mud that way...
There are those who will say may
Some of them, will kneel and pray.

Why should I go, but I must go any way.
Our weapons firefight both night and day.
I watch men die in every way,
They're all so young, I hear some say:

The game of war, not fun to play,
A bigger toll it takes each day
So many die, in the sun they lay.
The price of freedom, with lives they pay.

How many men, must they slay.
Before the sad, again are gay,
How long will it be, that must stay...
This war make no sense any way.

Nguyen Phuong

INVITED

Afternoon rain
wets your dress
on your way home
That's how we met
It rains
on a summer day
and where you live
is so far away
You stand all alone
in a fray
I have asked
I have invited
Why do you not want to stay?

My place -
small enough
to keep you dry
My heart -
small enough
to make you smile.

Vietnamese poem "*Mời*"
English version by PHẠM NGỌC

Nguyen Phuong

MY LIFE BESIDE YOU

Is thirty years seem so long?
Oh no!
Still deeply owed
Still deeply loved
Thirty years
Murky cloud
Windy days
Rainy sways
Seasons come and go
But our life together
Is here to stay
Every sunrise, every twilight
The memories we shared
Still glowing bright
Like a rose just blooms
You are always
Fresh in my mind
And your life besides me
As beautiful as a blue sea
Another thirty years,
Thirty years of true love
It will be!!!

Vietnamese poem "*Đời Ta Bên Em*"
English version by PHẠM NGỌC

Flowers of Love - 54

Ho Mong Thiep

THE TRAIN WHISTLE

There is a railroad not far from where I dwell;
The night train wails within listening distance.
Its whistle in my remembrance recalls well
My dad's eager dream throughout his existence.

At least once he yearned, by his ardor urged,
To ride an express train from South to North
Right after the country from hostilities emerged,
To revisit old beautiful sceneries henceforth.

Alas, one day he deceased, still discontent,
Leaving behind the modest wish yet not come true.
But, were he to live unto this day of no consent,
He would feel each night more grief so undue.

What of the world that exceeds the irony bitter
If not that upon the end of all firing and dying
The crowds had to rush and seek refuge hither,
Crossing the risky ocean, any dangers defying.

Ho Mong Thiep

Here, I have been longing and will still wait
For a glorious return from this exile line,
For his sake to realize his reverie, though late,
To contemplate again the landscapes in the shine.

Yes, to admire the divinely splendid country
Where ancesters'd drawn swords since foundation,
Setting bright examples of national recovery
To dutiful heirs of that non-severable nation.

But there each night the train whistles and wails
Since the railroad is close to where I reside.
As steel wheels are rolling on chill steel rails,
Its whistle rends my heart with nostalgia inside.

Vietnamese poem "*Tiếng Còi Xe Lửa*"
English version by THANH THANH

Ho Mong Thiep

PICTURESQUE FOR EVER

You inquired after me, while in exile, into my sand:
Whether I have ever felt missing our motherland,
Pitied and regretted the abundance of the past,
When the peaceful sun everywhere was shining fast?

Yes, be it picturesque for ever the countryside!
With kites flying over the far end of the dyke,
White storks walking alongside many a rice field,
Some flute herding buffaloes home so sweet a yield.

Narrow roads, green bamboo hedges surrounding,
Rows of arecas swaying in the fresh wind mounting,
The ferry-sampan reflecting in the water its image,
Rice-pestling songs echoing in the moonlit village.

And admiring the immense universe, those times,
While tasting scented tea we composed our rhymes,
Pervaded with the flavor of our native place,
Both souls leavened under the starred space.

Ho Mong Thiep

But, at present, one at stay, the other at large,
Our separation is on my heart a resentful charge.
You, unfortunate, have gotten caught in damnation,
And 1, though free, involved in human situation.

I am afraid of twilight, of shadows of night,
Of time arousing more and more grief in my plight.
Oh, homeland, relatives and friends, no assistance
Of any eagle could bridge so infinite a distance!

Vietnamese poem *"Muôn Đời Diễm Tuyệt"*
English version by THANH THANH

TyNa

IN REPLY TO YOUR POEM

Inspired by a poem by the Chinese poet Truong Tich with
the following verse: "Thou know that I am already married.."

Footprints on the moony paths have not yet faded
Yellow roses are still in bloom by the brooklet.
Knowing that I'm already married,
You reveal your deep feelings as a lonesome poet.
To your affections I was never ever indifferent
Just ... blown with the wind of time like a flower.
Your touching poem overflows with love, attachment
Facing the mirror , I feel now sour and bitter.
Hiding sighs , I manage to give pretty smiles daily
Hope you always understand I have my own family.
Since long all the ups and downs through time
Have I shared with the life partner of mine .
Understanding you , I'd like to visit you soon
But our hearts remain
as pure as the bright full moon.
Cherry leaves cease not falling down outside
At your return spring has gone by.
Still admiring you - my -ex-schoolmate,
for your talent, goodness

TyNa

Nothing however can loosen the family tie
Keep memories of those days, so dear so priceless
Regret not being side by side till the day we die.
I covertly knit the eyebrows while you sadly frown
Praying for forgetting each other
is all love can do now.
My home from yours is obviously no distance
Why seem so far as two ends of a river ?
We still behold the same sun each day - no difference !
You and my spouse are such good friends as ever.
Why none can lighten the pains you've gone through ?
When I crossed the other road without you -
With appreciation, I 'd reply to you sincerely
My true joy means the happiness of my family.
May you marry soon
with the true one you'll meet and cherish
So that we all realize
our true love really ... finally perish.

Tonight,
rain drops and autumn breezes are singing a duet,
Asking the neighbor's shadow:
why not rest down yet? ...

TyNa

A POEM FOR AN EX-SCHOOLMATE
(LOVE OF MUTUAL UNDERSTANDING)

Knowing that you've enjoyed a good marriage
peacefully
It's a slight comfort to this love of mutual
understanding.
Oh dear My Nuong of Truong Chi, every night sadly(1)
You can still hear the bamboo flute whispering ?
I wonder if the pretty girl of the humble West village(2)
Still can recall olden days
of washing silks by a cottage.
Miss Yang, heavenly beauty among the royal ladies(2)
Still waiting for your admirer
to bring you favorite lychees ?
In romantic moonlight,
contemplating fragrant flowers by now
Dieu Thuyen,
how can you forget your promise and vow ? (2)
I'm like the Giang-Chau Mandarin,
one night on a river of willows (3)

TyNa

Playing music now
merely enhances burdens of sorrows,
Once truly said from the heart bottom :
" I'm in love with you"

I perpetually engraved all that,
why no dreams come true! ?
I foster remembrance of you
like Son Ba misses Anh Dai (4)
Wherefore you choose
to walk your way with Ma van Tai ? (4)
Looking forward to sailing with you
along the Dream River
But your boat has anchored somewhere else,
how bitter !
Blue bird has flied away to floating clouds above,
Leaving me here alone with the everlasting first love.
Since young school times,
we've understood and admired each other
Why are we not destined
to become loving life partners ?

TyNa

Our story ends
like old tales about the hero and the beauty
Never found to be together
because of the jealous Destiny !
Now I can only blame myself and feel happy,
When seeing your family in delightful harmony.
If we cannot enjoy happiness, glory together
We shall silently share all sadness of life forever...
* * *

My dear Princess Huyen Tran so far away, out of sight (5)
Do you know the loyal General Tran misses you
tonight?(5)

(1) Truong Chi and My Nuong : a tragic love story in Vietnamese
    literature
(2) Tay Thi, Miss Yang, Dieu Thuyen : 3 of the 4 distinguished
    beautiful women in the Chinese history of all times
(3) Giang Chau Mandarin designated Tu Ma Giang Chau author of Ti Ba
    Hanh , a well known masterpiece in Chinese literature..
(4) Son Ba, Anh Dai, Ma van Tai : characters of a noted Chinese love
    story.
(5) Huyen Tran , General Tran: a well-known love story in Vietnamese
    historical legends.

TyNa

SHADOW TALKING

By the still Mirror Lake in a chilly night, how solitary !
I stroll all alone, counting every pace of cares and
anxiety.
The yellow moon begins to dim,
grayish clouds to thicken
Frail dew drops sprinkle all over rustling trees
- night is forsaken.
At tripping over unseen barriers on the life journey daily,
I'm aware of no escape from the boundless jail for me.
I face the Mirror Lake, my shadow looks at me:
- Deep in the gloomy night, why are you here so lonely ?
  Life of hard struggles has not yet ended , my dear
  Your moaning sighs by the lake, who can ever hear ?
- Oh shadow, only you could understand thoroughly
  Can arduous efforts ever move the indifference of the
  Almighty ?
  Carrying at start good will of helping ,
  striving for justice
  Yet midway one's tasted disappointments,
  bitter prejudice!

TyNa

Shadow says:
- Patiently sham ignorance,
  Keep being good at endurance.
  The declining sun naturally sets in the west
  Toil of changing that is indeed useless, not best .
  It's wiser to lie in the dark, watching fluctuations
  Keep eyes keen, ears sharp to comprehend all situations
  The more discouragements ,
  the harder your iron will should be
  The longer, it takes.,
   the more modest soul it will guarantee -
  Golden dragons are still hiding in stagnant waters,
  self training
  Phoenixes are taking shelter in deep jungles,
  waiting for spring
  "Have no spite against the Heaven upper,
   Bear no hatred for the earthly world or whoever"
  Keep noble spirits as high mountains, so topless
  Human life simply lasts one hundred years more or less
  Till the last breath , keep mind peaceful and stainless.

Let's smile at life that's turned upside down
Break grief into pieces by laughing away all sorrow
and frown...

Do Huu

EVENING MELODY

Quite a chance that day the journey was granting,
On our long way, the afternoon sun slanting.
Over the wind your singing voice took dominion
To lull human life's vicissitudes to oblivion.
What scenery! with smoke your eyes dimming,
The vast country over with tune was brimming.
Suddenly I reminisced about our motherland
So far that albatrosses hardly reach its strand.
Your hair was bob-waving against the stream;
Your lips ambitiously showed such a beam.
All at once I felt as though I had become of yore
In contrast with your prime of life in the core...
Then comes this journey you're out of my sight
And my way seems endless in the starlight.
How I miss you along each mile of wishing hot
Wondering if you still remember or simply forgot.

Vietnamese poem "*Nhạc Chiều*"
English version by THANH THANH

Flowers of Love - 66

Vu Hoi

OH,
MY DEAR SIMPLE STATUE

Oh, my dear simple statue
Shedding tears, the sky, not blue,
Swiftly running from your eyelids,
Staring eyes, eternal clouds.

Oh, my dear simple statue,
Shadows stretching, shades of woe,
Sadness dancing in your garments
Autumn leaves cling to your dress.

Tears are dropping, rain is pouring
Down your cool and stony cheek.
Simple, white and all-embracing
Love surrounds me with regret.

Oh, my dear simple statue,
Gentle winds caress your hair.
Hair cascading while you dream
And smile without a sign of mirth.

Vu Hoi

Oh, why, my dear simple statue
Hide within the still of night?
And looking down, not see the boy
Who waits to hear a statue's voice.

Oh – tell him of his Motherland
Of sweat-stained sand, and hate, and love,
And tell him of his place of birth,
And bind his wounded heart with grace.

Oh, why, my dear statue, simple
And senseless to the chill of night,
Aren't you amazed when sunlight comes
And still you weep the tears of darkness?

So – Mourning is the statue's game.
No sounds of joy, instead you weep.
The teardrops fall, you sob and mourn.
Your feet are ankle-deep in tears.

Though you are a breathless stone
And may you stand forever, dear,
You have no soul, and yet you would
Make me,

       A poet,

           Fall into a bad mood.

Vu Hoi

TO MISS LIBERTY

Please, show me
A street
So far named Liberty,
Now called Insurrection.
Please, show me Saigon Post Office
To send Her
A letter
About a love story
That I've kept grieving over the years
For a broken promise.

I am a person
Losing his mother
During the war
And bearing forever
The sorrow of that misfortune.

I happened to be wondering in the streets
In my gloomy days,
I happened to feel a distance between you and me
Although we both live in our very country
(And not on a foreign land!)

Vu Hoi

Miss Liberty!
Please come back
To make people see again smiles on faces,
And me, the lustrous black my hair once had,
And to make the first kiss
Remain eternal on the lips.
My arms will hug you
To sinking in dreams
And the first kiss
Will stay forever on the lips.

Vietnamese poem *"Gửi Nữ Thần Tự Do"*
English version by THU VAN

Nguyen Phan Nhat Nam

SCOWL NO MORE, DARKENING CLOUDS

Scowl no more, darkening clouds.
Cast away your leaden brows.
For my love is coming, to me.

Rush not, you I beseech:
Let my words of love on your downy wings roam
Until the end of the universe.

Deprive me not of the enchanting smile on her lips
And the lovely eyes that house a thousand dreams.
Drench her not with your torrential vehemence,
For blame me she would, sulking for an eternity.
Shake not the golden leaves of their branches,
Or count them I would, at the end of the lane.

Nguyen Phan Nhat Nam

Oh how intently I listen to every footstep;
Fervently I pray, hers it be, please.
But my love she chooses to play with my heart;
So here I stand, forlorn, in the waning light,
Watching the gilded glory dying on yon cottages,
Listening to the tune that greets the afternoon breeze.
Faint and slow it is, as the beatings of my heart.

Desert me not, fading light.
Let me wait a little while would you please.
Delay for a moment the descending mantle of the night,
And the quickening shadow of my heart.

Vietnamese poem *"Thôi Đừng"*
English version by PHAN THI BACH NGA

Nguyen Phan Nhat Nam

SOMETIME IT'S SO

Sometimes it shines,
'Cause it's not raining.
Sometimes in bloom yon flamboyants burst
'Cause it's the end of summer.

That maiden of mine,
By a bridge over the waters abides.
Queen of my heart and my dreams she stays.

'Twas at the Spring Fair,
By the stream we met.
Shy and lovely in her new dress,
My soul enthrall did she.

There at my threshold she stood,
One September full moon,
A vision dear to my heart ever since.

Sometimes she whispers-soft and low,
To me, and to me alone,
That it's forever. Yes, forever.

Nguyen Phan Nhat Nam

Sometimes she gazes into my eyes,
Sweetly - to me, and to me alone,
Saying, it's forever. Yes, forever.

Forever she'll be mine.
And together we'll build our little nest.
Together we'll be, forever.

I love the tiny boat that crosses the stream.
I love the old town that watches her grow.
I love every step of the way she walks.
And you sure know why it's so.

Sometimes my heart's filled with happiness
'Cause my love by my side stays.
'Cause, look, lingering on her tresses
The last sunlight of the day.

Vietnamese poem "Có Khi"
English version by PHAN THI BACH NGA

Huong Nam

MY VIETNAMESE DRESS: "AO DAI"

When I first came to the U.S.A.,
I put my Vietnamese dress away,
*Wondering: "Is it weird to wear **ao dai** here?"*

*My **ao dai** has two flaps very light,*
As the long wings of a swallow-tail,
Flying into my dream of white clouds
and American blue sky,
A feeling of freedom and fresh love!

My blood stream ran fast and my heart warmer,
Waking me in that morning summer,
Falling free and very happy!

*I wore my **ao dai** walking to temple,*
Stepping gently as a bird singing in the tree,
Some Americans looked at me,
Smiled, and said: "You look pretty!"
Did they praise the dress or the person?
Either way, still it must be,
They are a generous people,
In this freedom country!

Huong Nam

OVER-FEELING

I heard
Very tiny sounds from the earth
As the turning of magma,
Or the noise of dew dropping on leaves,
Or the voice of insects trembling in the dark yard.

Yes! For a long time I have listened
Sounds smaller than a strand of hair,
In the silence of deep oceans,
In the vast shadow of nights,
In the earth's core or the unlimited sky...

Is there something touching lightly then leaving,
As ultra micro waves
or extraordinary ideas delicate and very bright?
They seem like the pure quintessence
Of angels, of elite spirits, of aliens...
Or are they merely human minds?
Lighter than a soft breath!
Quicker than a heart beat!
Although invisible, meeting for just a little while,
But giving deeply: consciousness, emotion,
And precious loving...

Huong Nam

SMALL, NO-NAME BOATS

There were thousands of boats,
On the way to be free,
They paid the price,
With their lives and property,
Disappearing into the seas.
Those boats were not famous like the Titanic!
They were very small and weak,
But they carried many people,
Healthy boys and pretty girls...
All died!
Before they had learned about loving freely,
Before they could think and willingly sacrifice,
Before the boats were engulfed.
The men sank just as they began to fight,
And women were raped until they died!
There were no lights,
no food,
no drinking water...
Not even a drop for their lives.

Huong Nam

So many died silently in the ocean!
Oh! Small unnamed boats,
Buried in the seas,
As little fishes die desperately,
Killed by the bigger ones,
by toxic spill,
by the scourge of El Nino...
On the way to be free!

Le Trong Nghia

SUCH IS LIFE

I met her on a beautiful day!
I said hi to her
She said hi to me
I talked to her
She talked to me
I like her
She likes me
I love her
She loves me
We love each other
I proposed to her
She said yes
We got married on a cheerful day
7hen we have problems
She doesn't talk to me
I don't talk to her
We won't listen to each other
We quarrel a lot everyday
We ended up in a divorce
Our happy marriage has ended
But lives are still going on
It is a fact of life
Such is life!

Le Trong Nghia

A DAY OF SPRING

I wake up early this morning
I hear the birds singing
In the garden, the dew is dropping
7he dawn begins
The wonderful day of Spring
Through the windows
7he sunlight beams are dancing
Around me and within the room
Indicating the beautiful day
will be starting soon
Smelling the freshness of dawn
Reminds me of the scents of her hair
I told myself no matter where
Some day I'll find her and tell her
How much I care!
I wish that she could hear
7he voice of my heart
which is saying,
"I love you, my dear!

Le Trong Nghia

FAREWELL TO MOTHER TERESA & PRINCESS DIANA

We shall never forget
The months of August and September
In the year of nineteen ninety seven
We lost the two greatest ladies on earth
Mother Teresa, mother of the world
Princess Diana, princess of the world

How great you both were
We all thank you both
For what you have taught us
What does love mean?
Love means to care
Love means to share
Love means to console
No matter who
No matter where
Now you have gone
But your divine souls
Are always in our hearts
Tears filled my eyes
To bid farewell and good bye
To the two greatest ladies
That we respected and admired?
Mother Teresa and Princess Di.

Trac Pham

NIGHT

It's late, too late indeed
Too late to work or think
Too late for all, except to sink
Into the oblivion of sleep
And lot the daily gripes reap
A harvest of frustration, fear and grief

The night is warm
Yet, it warms not me, entangled in a net
Of trouble, anxiety, distress
And harassment, anguish, hate
But isn't it already too late to look for the
daylight's peep?

There is no escape from life
In work, in play, everything is strife
Who are the real friends
who can help me with deeds
And lift me from this bottomless pit!

Paul Cao

A CUP OF COFFEE

Why did you do that?
How dare you make me sad?

Waiting for you every morning,
It's me – yes, it's only me!
    And you, sitting at the old corner, drinking coffee,
    Listening to the folk
    Singing, you "make" smoke...

Through the small hidden window,
I looked at you slyly.
As habit as the sun rises
Every morning,
You come into my shop with the same "boring" face.
My shop seems like yours,
That corner especially
You're used to "use",
Secretly...I think of you.
But the "strange customer" never heeds...to me
Who has nice looking eyes as blue as sky,
Who has shining hair as fair as a lyre.
Not knowing how to do, how to share,
When I am just a girl,
A girl just waits for you
Who would have a glance to me;

Paul Cao

To me speak something please!
Something's not a long story, but I'd see...
"a signal from you"
I wait...and you stay!
"This song" repeats every day!

And now, even my eyes are openly maximized,
I can't help my silent sights...
The wind blows you here;
Sitting on the table, you have no lonely ear;
With a girlfriend, first time I see you charm your dear!
A cup of coffee's brought to you painfully,
A mistake I make unusually
Toppling coffee
As if my heart falling deeply...
It happens so quick, make me confused, "I'm sorry,
first time, I have a mistake, please forgive me!"

There are many shops you can date.
There are many places you can wait.
How come you choose my old place?
Make me hate my own fate!

It's finished, stops my mute love,
And dries my dreamy cove!
Who tries to crumple a "cloudy rose"?
And understands my rainy soul?

Paul Cao

FAITHFULNESS
(To My Wife)

Which love is the most faithful of all?
Adam and Eve!
Because they were the only two
That crossed the threshold of life.
And from that creation,
There is another…

…my love to you!

Kim Phuong Tran

CLOSE YOUR EYES AND ACT AS ONE HUMAN RACE

Different in color, different in mind
What's really different is just through your eyes
Deep from inside we are alike...
Just flesh and blood that there inside
What can you say about our outsides
When we are just human alike
You have a heart and so do I
Why don't you search it for better advice.

Your heart to love, your mind to think !
Just open it and accept their being
No one can just be like you or I
We all come from different background and family life
Accept everyone for who they are...
Through not what you see
But what you know inside
Just close your eyes and act as one human race

Kim Phuong Tran

VALENTINE TO SHARE

Valentine is here and there.
Bringing the love for us to share.
Give a smile, make it last.
Shake my hand and forgive all that has passed.
There is not much that I could say...
Just a little wish of joy and cheer.
For the day of love is here.
And to say a simple word...
Like "Thanks a lot, foe always being there".
For being a special person in my heart.

Le Van Ba

BLACK STONE WALL
THE HEROES' MONUMENT

(To all warriors who died in the Vietnam War)

How recollecting the black stone wall is!
How reminding the heroes' monument is!
Your souls enjoy in the heaven
Your names always bright on this Earth
Standing motionless Lincoln says, "Hi" to you
Sky high, Washington sends flowers
The Capitol Hill praises your duty
Your reputation flashing everywhere
The warriors of Liberation engraved in History
The heroes of the Vietnam War
will transcribe in the future
Your bodies kept under green grasses
Your good reputation flying on the National Park
An evening fall, putting a wreath of red flowers
For remembering you from the bottom of my heart
Remembering fire and cannon-ball on the Old Citadel
Mourning year of the Monkey!
Khe Sanh forest rain and wind

Le Van Ba

On Washington, clouds flying over stone monument
All the world, bring tears on the eyes of your comrades
So many teenagers, innocently step and step
Step forward on your road and wave our flags
Now scent and smoke spreading over
Our life and death run parallel in the old battlefields
Remembering grass fields, rice fields
Edge of the forests, corner of the towns
We have to go on our guard
We have to keep on our duty
In the sky the Eagles flit
On the open sea, the boats glide
With great one, we act freely in
Air space, Territorial waters
We have the same happiness or misery
Though stone of Five Elements Mountains not engrave
Though leaves of Long Mountains, bring no success
Your merits are very high and very deep
Your blood and bones were sacrificed
Old man looking for old friends with glassy eyes
Young women remembering their fathers,
choked with tears
Young men reading your names with all respects

Le Van Ba

They proudly step up in line of hero
Gifts from grandchildren and the group of students
Gifts from friends are many kinds of flowers
Some crowns of flowers are still fresh
They are the precious gifts to you
A few matches, a few packs of cigarettes
Keeping the warriors warm on cold nights
Some pictures of battlefield were smudged
Ten violet letters of some love stories incomplete
Some people paid all that they had loaned from you
Debts, gamble debts could be paid off
But debts of emotion, how can they pay off
Cloud forms, mountain shadows are infinite
Life is uncertain, time gathered and gone
Present life, you are heroes of the Free World!
Next life you will be the Angels in the Heaven
I am happy, for you have beautiful tombs
I am said, for Vietnam is still in ruin
The cemeteries for Vietnam warriors are deserted
Their souls wandering in the dark sky
Clouds flying and flying as their souls do
Winds howling and howling
as their spirits hold on the trees
Stopping, visiting my old friends
With all respects from the bottom of my heart.

Le Van Ba

ON A RIVER
REMEMBERING OTHERS

Mississippi in my mind is very imposing
Why is it a tiny spring?
How stagnant its currents are!
Oh! Shallow river with bushes
From near and far sandy mount snow covering
And under the bridge hanging icy wires
At the City Hall, the Golden Horse is looking upward
He remembers the race, the large family in Europe
Stopping, looking down and gazing the river
It seems that from the bottom of water current
The Indian images were appeared vaguely
They were fondling some crops of sweet corns
I get up, all its green to heaven's vault
Flying, there are so many wild ducks
By ten thousand lakes spreading to the horizon

Le Van Ba

Oh! Water birds!
Who invites you to this Spring Festival
Mississippi running about thousand miles
It rests at Saint Louis City
And calls the friend named Missouri
They converging and running to Memphis
Mississippi! Trees and meadows
Missouri! Flood and flow
They running into the open sea
Mexico Gulf is very blue
How clear this river is! The towns reflect in water
How high the river banks are!
The plains running to the heaven
A beautiful river! A rich nation!
The cruises carry the passengers to Paradise
Seeing Mississippi! As soon as my tears bursted
Remembering the Dong Nai! Ben Nghe!
Song Con Rivers
Remembering the milking river Mekong
When do I come back and take a bath in them.

Thu Minh

ME AND THE SEA

Today, though, I became a stranger to the sea:
As a stopping-off sightseer, it didn't know me.
Over there, heaving sails were going far-away,
And down there, ripples whispering in calm play.

This scenery was so quiet that I wonder why
Only myself was to face the sea and the sky.
Only myself face-to-face with life had to deal:
Even each little wish faded out, in pain to feel.

Why the sea was in peaceful state, yet, while
I felt my heart a whole of fire screaming isle
To burn into thin air all of my dreams and hope
So that along a restless life my way I'd grope
Fragile like a butterfly's wing. Prospect: nope!

Vietnamese poem *"Tôi Và Biển"*
English version by THANH THANH

Tran Tinh Nhu

SEA FLOWER

Overhearing the "Sea Flower" song
Reminds me of our youth story so strong,
When hurrying clouds covered Saigon Capital
To share a couple's farewell in the "Fall".

Your trip brought you to the blue sea
On a staggering ship through foamy waves.
Standing in the vast open under the high sky
Did you pick up a fresh "White Flower" for me?

Times and times when the sun sank on deserted beach
My footprints here and there on sand... you searched.
Indifferent waves,
however, had erased our traces of love
Leaving in the dusk only melancholy swallows chirps.

In the last letter to me, you said:
Sitting aboard, I am watching night stars,
The milky way that's glittering afar.
My combat uniform, ceaseless rain suddenly wets.

Tran Tinh Nhu

Does the cold come from salted water
or somewhere else?
Because I can't see you this July,
Through gentle sea breeze and beautiful moonlight
Renovating my vow, best wishes for your Birthday, I said

My Birthday is on the same day of "Nguu Chuc Nu"
Our meeting is like a crenate and water, gathering
Anywhere I live... I always think of you and dispersing
While telling myself... "Birdwings are still tireless."

This is the sea blue color you liked before
The color I dressed to see you whom I adored.
On crystal sand... I drew my future life
Hoping to live together,
shedding our shadows under moonlight.
Actually we don't have that crystal blue of seawater now
When leaving lovely souvenirs behind.
Let's hope for the peaceful day with calm waves
and gentle breeze,
When we altogether come back in our ancestor land
and happily live.

Nguyen Nguyen Thanh

JESUS RESURRECTED

This evening I searched my way to God's range
Where they were celebrating Easter, his morale.
There I found the one familiar but now strange:
That was you who had strayed into the chorale.

We did not recognize one another at this hour
Everything God had reserved the right to oversee.
Your ventricles were saturated in God's power,
Not a tiny cavity in your heart was saved for me.

I waited for you at the gate in front of the church
With a glimmer of my hope I kindled a candle;
But you had already dissolved in the lambs herd;
I returned into the night my loneliness to handle.

God has taught his disciples: thou open thy heart
To love thy fellow humans all to live in chime.
Well, my heart is able only to love her, how tart!
Oh Lord, but does she love me right at this time?

Jesus was resurrected and you were too tonite
I wondered if tomorrow to revert you would deem
To recognize in life with vicissitudes though trite
One another, ourselves, after the paradise dream.

Vietnamese poem *"Chúa Phục Sinh"*
English version by THANH THANH

Flowers of Love - 96

Pham Thuong Hop

THE BLIND CHILD

Where have you come from, poor creature?
Emaciated and ragged is the most striking feature!
With hoarse voice your songs sound without hope;
With your shaking stick your way on you grope.
Within your reach is the vacant pitch dark;
Your begging murmur shows the suffering mark
Beside human forms similar to statues carved:
Oh my God!
Who would read
You have since long starved?
Who would pay heed
To your broken-hearted cry?
As you are indifferently looked at by passers-by...

Vietnamese poem *"Em Bé Mù"*
English version by THANH THANH

Luu Tran Nguyen

INTIMATE SENTIMENTS OF LEAF

Everything will be desolated finally,
Like the end of the party.
I'm the green leaf living on the tree,
Also destroyed by autumn's authority.

Don't blame me for leaving too soon,
It's better for me to cede the place to bud rising,
I am too old to be green,
And young life is needed for everyone.

Looking down at my tiny roots awhile,
I see flowers crying, regretting their short life,
Who knows, from far away, millions of butterflies,
A storm's coming, they'll die.

And the ants are fighting for food wildly,
Narrow-minded like their own destiny.
I vomit thinking about deracinated enemies,
Just animals wearing human clothes, dirtily.

Luu Tran Nguyen

I'm the leaf with a soul as innocent as your eyes,
Watching God creating men, I smile.
They look like ants and dirty flies,
Full of ambition and spite.

Finally, everything will be gone
Like the end of the party will be none.
Why does one regret always something lost,
Then, forget that happiness forever will come?

Luu Tran Nguyen

THE POOR SHADOW

I wandered in the garden,
Looking for a leaf fallen.
There were so many yellow leaves.
The leaf that I want, I couldn't see

I wandered in the night,
Looking for a light.
There were billions of glow - worms,
The light that I want, vanished with storm.

I wandered my whole life,
Running after a shadow I couldn't find.
Then, everything has gone,
I'm still alone.

One day, coming back to my homeland,
I see a leaf on her hand,
And two bright lights looking at me, happily,
She, the poor shadow I found, finally.

Dien Linh Le Khac Ly

NOCTURNAL JUNGLE

Coiled in morning cloud, trees sniveling,
Creek or silver tear stream gushing,
Inclined a half moon contorted with weep,
Is sorrow for only one human being?

Flowers of Love - 101

Tina Thanh Huong

MY KIND OF GUY!

He is nice
He is a little shy
He is all right
He is a little slow
He takes his time
But he is kind
He smiles most of the time
He's contents with his life
He has a good heart
He is a good guy
He always think nice
Of everyone !
He is easy to please
Easy to talk to
Easy to listen
He is really a gentleman

Tina Thanh Huong

HE'S OK!

I met him one day
I spilled coffee on his suit
I didn't know what to say
I was embarrassed
I looked very sad
He said, it's ok !
Coffee was very hot
I am glad, he's all right
The fifteenth of May
It was his birthday
We went out to celebrate
At his favorite place
He turned fifty five
few white hairs on his sides
He looks fine for his age
He has a creative life

Diem Thy

ONCE UPON A TIME

Once upon a time, there was one in violet clad
To continue inspiring my poetic dreams so sad.
Until times later on, Cupid would never deign!
He is so sparing in grace for me to await in vain.
Clouds to drift, lovers to part, life is like to make;
I have experienced many a turn my heart to ache.
Sadness's choked me with compassion and stays!
Oh darling, how I miss the violet in by-gone days!

Vietnamese poem *"Nghìn Xưa"*
English version by THANH THANH

Nam Giao

GOODBYE

The broken love faded away as we said goodbye
She, like the shadow, through the bridge, passing by
Went far away and left me all alone in this melancholy
town
Waiting silently for her under the declined moon in
late night...

Vietnamese poem " *Vẫy Tay*"
English version by PHẠM NGỌC

Huynh Ngoc Diep

NOSTALGIA

Heart like the falling leave on the door's step
Sorrows in me have aged as the wind-swept
Suddenly I missed the full moon of yesteryear
It has been gone since you are no longer near...

Vietnamese poem "*Nhớ*"
English version by PHẠM NGỌC

Flowers of Love - 106

Huynh Ngoc Diep

SADNESS

It seems that it is raining in the street,
The autumn wind causing dead leaves to fall,
And some bad memories sadder than a grief
On the autumn dawn to impregnate my soul

Vietnamese poem *"Nỗi Buồn"*
English version by THANH THANH

Nguyen Thi Khanh Minh

MOUNTAIN TRANSFORMED

Since you have become the faraway sea
Mountain sings the crater's song
Listen to the miracle of ashes
Transformed into the whitecap
Searching for a place to belong

Vietnamese poem "*Hóa Thân Núi*"
English adaptation by PHẠM NGỌC

Flowers of Love - 108

FOR EACH OTHER

Tomorrow if we have to part
I will keep the memories of my youth
for the long roads that I travel
and I still peacefully love you

Tomorrow if we are further apart
I will dream in my sorrow
Even all the unmeaningful things
Still become parts that I am missing

Tomorrow if the world comes tumbling
Lead me to anguish separation
Even so! Please for each other
Let's love until the end of the desperation

Vietnamese poem *"Vì Nhau"*
English version by PHẠM NGỌC

Flowers of Love - 109

Nguyen Thuy Linh

THE WHITE CLOUD
IS STILL FLYING

And... Since then...
When the Spring comes in strange land
In the poetry I was a vagrant
I often advise myself
Hey!...Sea and Cloud...
Do you still go back on the old way?
Along the roads the bamboo's ramparts get their
shades
The hamlet's small way
The rocky ascent's top where we passed
In the late afternoon with light sunlight
I think of...far away...
Where are you now ?..
Winter passed and Spring too...
Is there sunny in Swayrieng and Tan Phu...
Is there the rain fall down

Nguyen Thuy Linh

The voice is here...
I look up at the thinly cloud...stand alone and sing
As I am staying in my dream and look above
Whose white dress...be as like as...
...The cloud in sky
I cultivate the love's feeling and call my old flame...
Though that The Heaven changes the sunny and
replaces the rain...
As to me...I will never forget and change.

Nguyen Van Cuong

INSPIRED BY THE WIND

The wind blew up your long dress lap
After school against your body full of sap:
Returned home, I got sick many at night.

The white cloth stuck on your breast tight
Much thinner than the pall of stray rain:
Back home, I stayed in bed and in pain
Enduring a fever many and many a days.

In the pagoda each time I heard you pray
To the Buddha, and the sutras deployed,
I though I had already Nirvana enjoyed.

And at last the evening you were married
Into peace of mind I got the toast carried.

But, that time, feeding your baby blest,
I caught sight of you, with all bare breast:
I felt my body in feverish ripples buried...

Vietnamese poem "*Viết Từ Cơn Gió*"
English version by THANH THANH

I HAVE LEFT BEHIND

I have left my children to save my own hide
While I could not have prepared them for life
With their kids nobody knows what would betide
To their future and towards which how to strive.

I have left my property that from sweat flowed
But the thugs appropriated and refused to return.
They claimed over my body the debt never-owed,
And the sharp practices they forced me to learn.

I have left my poor people unfortunate and unable
Wiped out of intelligence and wise scrutinies,
In a war-torn country which the traitors disable,
Squandering resources and missing opportunities.

I have left behind my past but not for it to pass
Because I never forget or deny its persistence.
To head for a better tomorrow I have to amass
All experiences that are part of my existence.

I have left them for this land of promises full,
And advantageous for my dreams to come true
Not only to free myself, out of miseries to pull,
But also to claim for my compatriots their due.

Thanh Thanh

LAUD TO POPE JOHN PAUL II

I laud you for most of the other moral systems detecting
And for anything true and holy in them not rejecting -
Those Asian Buddhist, Confucian, and Taoist religions,
And Australian hundreds-of-centuries-old native
traditions.

I commend you for admitting your predecessors
misapprehended
The earth's form and position for which Galileo
contended.
To deny the roundness and movement of the globe,
in error
The Inquisition persecuted the physicist, inflicted terror!

I praise you for acknowledging that, without lenience,
In order to liberate Jerusalem from Islamic obedience,
They fostered crusades in the European Catholics' name,
But they had recourse to violence -unworthy of fame!

Thanh Thanh

*I admire you for testifying your anterior ones' lack of
truth
While love of one another is the Bible's thesis of "truth."
They considered black people slaves because of their
race,
And they tolerated, and even encouraged, slave trade!*

*I respect you for apologizing, to many a Latin nation,
For Spanish past roles in South-America Evangelization.
Delegated by the Church, Spain took advantage of the
situation
To practice cruelly massacre, tyranny, and exploitation!*

*I sympathize with your feeling about World War II a
sharp pain:
The Vatican's cooperation with the Nazis - a dark stain!
I am sorry for your yielding to the Vietnamese
protestation
Of their own countries prelacy against your ordination!*

*I love your getting prepared for the century twenty-first:
All predictions of the near end only mean a frenzy burst!
I extol your recognition of the processes of Evolution:
Such reasoning beyond Creation is quite a revolution!*

*I thank you for teaching Christians to repent of their sin
Committed in the past by certain Pontiffs and their kin.
Such lucidity, justice, and courage, of a man capable,
Lets me believe that you, the Pope, is not mistakable!*

Thanh Thanh

THE YEAR 2000

The year two thousand, I will be still alive,
And so will other animals and worms.
There still will be vegetables and germs,
And mundane life as ever, rain or shine.

Not the earth to stop revolving will tend,
Neither the seas to dry, nor the air to condense;
Each day will be a new one, not the last hence;
And the world - humanity - will face no end.

Wars will continue to erupt here and there
As an ordeal to test Man's thirst for Peace.
Poverty, ignorance, and diseases will not cease
For egoism, greed, and cruelty will not care.

But, anywhere on the globe, in any event,
There always will be conscience, common sense.
The elites still will vow the innocents' defense,
For people to be safe, prosperous, and content.

We still will have much more progress to make
And many more stars to explore and win.
To prepare for the twenty-first century to begin,
We need self-reliance striving for our own sake.

BIOGRAPHIES

NHU HOA LE QUANG SINH

Born May 21, 1929, in Quảng Điền, Triệu Phong, QuảngTrị Province, Central Vietnam; Former Lt. Colonel of the ARVN; member of Vietnamese Ex.Polictical Prisoner Association, The International Society of Poets; President of Sacramento Vietnamese Coalition; Founder and president of the Vietnamese Amateur Poets Society (VASP); Have part in CHTY (Flowers of Love Vietnamese Edition) volume I (95), II (96), III (97) and IV(98). Currently reside in Sacramento, California

NGUYEN PHUC SONG HUONG

Born 1941 in Hue, Central Vietnam. Member of the International Society of Poets, Thi Văn Cội Nguồn; Co-founder and General Secretary of The Vietnamese Amateur Poets Society. Have part in the anthologies of poems CHTY (Flowers of Love Vietnamese edition) volume I (95), II (96), III (97), IV (98); Gởi Người Dưới Trăng, Đường Xuôi Nẻo Ngược, Một Thời Lưu Lạc.(by Cội Nguồn). Publication: Thơ Vùng Tủi Nhục (in Vietnamese,1965), Among People (in English, 1995): Imprints For Posterity (in Vietnamese with Hoang Thanh, 1998)

THU VAN

Name Phạm Ngọc Nga; born in Pnom Penh, Kampuchia, grew up in Saigon; graduated from Faculty of Letters, Pedagogical Institute, Saigon with a BA degree in French, Master of Arts (MA) in French from George Mason University, USA. French teacher at Regina Mundi High, Saigon, Publication: Nắng Xuân (Sunny Spring) with Trình Xuyên - 1983; Have given lectures on Kim Vân Kiều, Aó Dài Việt Nam, Verses and Love (Lamartime); Have part in CHTY(Flowers of Love) Vol.3 - 97, Vol.4 - 98; currently reside in Richmond, Virginia.

LE SY DONG

Born November 21, 1938 in Saigon, Vietnam; Graduated with a degree (B.A) in Philosophy, Literature and Economy from Faculty of Letters. Former High School Principal; write short stories and poems published in Arts and Culture Magazines in Saigon before 1975. Have part in CHTY (Flowers of Love) Vol.1-95, Vol.2-96, Vol.3-97, Vol.4-98 Member of The International Society of Poets, Vietnamese Amateur Poets Society. Winner of the Diamond Homer Prize by Famous Poets Society 1995 and 1996; currently reside in Sacramento, CA.

PHAM NHA DU

Born in Bà Điểm, Gia Định, South Vietnam; former officer of the ARVN, English teacher at the Military Language School, Saigon before 1975. Currently working for Putman Investment Company in Boston, MA; member of the VAPS. Have part in CHTY (Flowers of Love) Vol. 2-96, Vol.3 - 97, Vol.4 -98. Reside in Dorchester, MA

CAO MY NHAN

Born in Sa-Pa, Hoàng Liên Sơn, North Vietnam, spent her childhood in Hải Phòng and Hà Nộii. Lived in Saigon before 1975, former officer of the ARVN; write verses at the age of 13. Have contributed to many anthologies of poems in Vietnam before 1975 and overseas after 1990. Currently reside in Lawndale, California.

NGUYEN THI SEN TRANG

Born in Đàlạt, Central Vietnam., Sen Trang grew up in the old Citadel city of Hue. Inheriting poetic nature of her hometown, the beautiful Hương River, the dreaming Ngự Mountain, and the rustic royal tombs, she has the romantic characteristic typical of Hue's lady. She is always searching for the truth, perfection and beauty though knowing that it hard to achieve. She also like to better herself and the living environment around her. Resettling in San Jose in September 1989, Sen Trang has worked for the International Rescue Committee to help resettle refugee in Santa Clara county since 1990.

PHAM NGOC

Family came from Thái Bình Province, North Vietnam; attended Falculty of Laws, Saigon; Resettled in California since 1975; currently working at STI Company in Palo Alto, California as a Process Engineer. Staff writer of Ngày Nay Magazine (Arizona), Contributing writer of Vietnam Times Magazine (California), Co-founder of Văn Tuyển Magazine (California). Member of VAPS; Have part in CHTY (Flowers of Love) Vol.2-96, Vol.3-97, Vol.4-98. Publication: Remembrance (with Nam Giao), The Place Where Love's Hiding (with 3 other poets), The Late Passion (Vietnamese poem-HAT 1998); Reside in Hayward, California.

PHAM TRUNG THANH

Born in Hải Phòng, North Vietnam. Fled the country with family to Hong Kong, confined in Hong Kong Camp for 8 years. Released on June 13, 1997; resettle in Begium November 1997. Currently reside in Brussels, Belgium.

LE NGUYEN

Born in Vỹ Dạ, Huế, Central Vietnam; former officer of the ARVN; Contributing writer to many newspapers in Saigon before 1975, Poems and articles published in the Magazines: Văn, Văn Học, Làng Văn, Thế Kỷ 21,Khởi Hành, Lý Tưởng, Cỏ Thơm, Hoa Sen, Văn Tuyển........; Have part in CHTY (Flowers of Love) Vol.3-97, Vol.4-98; have 20 poems set into music ; Publication: Rain Through Remembrance - 1997; Reside in Huntsville, Alabama.

VU DUC TO CHAU
Poet, Saigon, Vietnam

NGOC AN

Born in Vũng Tàu, South Vietnam; Write verses at school age. Contributed to many newspapers and magazines in Saigon before 1975 and several magazines in the US. Have part in many anthologies of poems in the California. Publication: Poetry As the Vibrant Notes of The Heart (1997); member of the Vietnamese Amateur Poets Society; Reside in San Jose, California

TRONG KHANH

Born in Tien Giang, South Vietnam; former teacher before 1975; Director of Travel and Tour agency in Sacramento, Cali. Publication: Tien Giang Poem Collection. Have part in CHTY (Flowers of Love) Vol. 1-95, Vol.2-86, Vol.3-97, Vol.4-98. Reside in Sacramento, California

NGUYEN PHUONG

Born in Hue, Central Vietnam. Have part in anthologies of poems CHTY (Flowers of Love) Vol.2-96, Vol.3-97 and other poem publication by Thi Đàn Lạc Việt and Cội Nguồn. Publication: Echoe From The Heart (Cội Nguồn -1997). Reside in San Jose, California

HO MONG THIEP

Born in Đà Nẵng, Quảng Nam Provice, Central Vietnam. He was a high-ranking civil servant in the goverment of the Republic of Vietnam, serving in Đà Nẵng, Vũng Tàu and Sàigòn After the fall of the R-VN he arrived in the States as a political refugee together with his family living around San Jose. Many of his poems were printed, read and well acclaimed in many cities and states. After his death, all his dispersed poems were gathered in one collection entitled " Ngàn Năm Gởi Mây Bay" (Fovever Gone with The Clouds) and published by his wife Agnes Ho who live in Milpitas, California

TyNa

Real name Bùi Tuyết Nga; born in Bến Ninh Kiều, Cần Thơ, South Vietnam; currently employed as a Process Technology Engineer; like music, poetry, cartoon film, traveling, arts and research ...Write poems and articles published in Vietnam Monthly Magazine, Vietnam Revue, Holland. Reside in Purmerend, Holland.

DO HUU

Born in Hue, Central Vietnam; graduated from Saigon University and San Jose State University; former teacher over 16 years; publication: Vietnamese Literature (Văn Chương Việt Nam, Sống Mới, Sàigòn 1972); The 50 Year History of The Buddhist Youth Association (GDPTVNHN) a volume of over 500 pages with color illustration; poems and articles printed in many Newspapers and Magazines. Currently Executive Director of Viet Bao USA, a daily newspaper in San Jose, California.

VU HOI

Pen name Hồng Khôi; born in Quảng Nam Province, Central Vietnam; Artist, Poet, Photographer; Founder of Painting-in-motion, Handwriting and Painting (Thư Họa); Painted portrait of Gen. Abrams, Commander in Chief of US force in S. Vietnam, 1972; Publication: Mùa Giao Cảm (A Season of Mutual Sympathy), poem, 1958; Hợp Tấu (Chorus); Member of International Pen Club, Vietnamese Amateur Poets Society; Honored with Kennedy's Prize in Painting 1962; Nominated for Biographical Inclusion in the ABJ's 5000 Personalities of the World, 1994. Reside in Rockville, MD.

NGUYEN PHAN NHAT NAM

Born in Sàigòn, South Vietnam; Resettled in US since 1994, attending Rancho Santiago College, Ca. Contribute writing to several newspapers and magazines in the US and Australia; Have part in CHTY (Flowers of Love) Vol.1-96, Vol.3-97, Vol.4-98; Special Prize Poetry Contest by Thi Đàn Lạc Việt, 1997; member of Vietnamese Amateur Poets Society; Reside in Garden Grove, Cali.

HUONG NAM

Born in Thủ Đức, South Vietnam; education: BS degree in Technology 1978; former Product Engineer, Frozen Goods Export Company, Saigon (78-81); Computer Programmer; Had activities in Literature and Arts at school age; have part in CHTY (Flowers of Love) Vol.3-97, Vol.4-98; several poems set to music by Việt Cường, Sỹ Thạc; Reside in Sacramento, California

LE TRONG NGHIA

Born in North Vietnam, evacuated to South Vietnam in 1954; former officer of the ARVN, graduated from The Infantry School Thủ Đức; Have part in CHTY (Flowers of Love) vol.2-96, Vol.3-97, Vol-4-98; Publication: Nhung Van Tho (The Rhymes, 1993), The Muse, 1996; Reside in Sacramento, California

TRAC PHAM
Engineer - Sacramento, California.

PAUL CAO

Born in Sàigòn, South Vietnam; Education: BA in Foreign Language, Pedagogical Institute 1983; BS, BA in Business Administration (Summa Cum Laude) 1-96 from Strayer College; Member of Vietnamese Amateur Poets Society. Have part in CHTY (Flowers of Love) Vol.1-95, Vol.2-96, Vol.3-97, Vol.4-98. Reside in Sterling, VA.

KIM PHUONG TRAN

Sacramento, California

LE VAN BA

Pen name Hoàng Duy; born in Bình Định, Central Vietnam; education: BA degree in Philosophy, Faculty of Letters, Saigon; Former officer of the ARVN; Publication: Nghìn Thu Xưa và Nay (Treatise, 1992); Poetic work: Tình Người Vượt Biên -91, Nữ Hoàng Tình Yêu - 92, Như Bóng Mây - 96, Bát Ngát Hương Đời -96; Have part in CHTY (Flowers of Love) Vol. 3-97, vol.4-98. Reside in Westminster, California

THU MINH

Real name Thu Minh Christine; born in Hà Nội, North Vietnam; Sound Technician for VNTV, Dance teacher; Second Prize of Dance Contest - Golden Pair of Shoes, 1991; Publication: Nhạc Lá (the Sound of Leaves 1998). Reside in Rochelle, France.

TRAN TINH NHU

Real name Trần Thị Nâu; born in Saigon, South Vietnam; Vietnamese Techer Lạc Hồng Vietanmese Language School, Sacramento; Have part in CHTY (Flowers of Love) vol3-97, Vol4-98; Reside in Sacramento, California.

NGUYEN NGUYEN THANH

Born in Hanoi, North Vietnam; Education: BA degree from Pedagogical Institute; Journalist; contributing writer to many newspapers and magazines in Vietnam; Editor in Chief of Tia Sáng Magazine (Germany); Have articles published in Thế Kỷ 21 and Văn Học Magazines, CHTY(Flowers of Love) vol3-97, Vol.4-98; Publication: Lửa Hồng Hoang (A Red Soliatry Flame-1996). Reside in Germany.

PHAM THUONG HOP

Real name Phạm Thị Hợp; born in Hải Phòng Province, North Vietnam. Former teacher. Fled the country to Hong Kong with a 10 year old child. Released from the camp in 1997; resettled in Brussels, Belgium.

LUU TRAN NGUYEN

Born in Hải Phòng, North Vietnam, evacuated to the South in 1954; former officer of the ARVN; Have part in CHTY (Flowers of Love) Vol.2-96, Vol.3-97, Vol.4-98; Publication:Mái Tóc Trầm Hương (Santal Hair - 1997); reside in Sacramento, California.

DIEN LINH LE KHAC LY

Born in Hương Trà, Thừa Thiên Province, Central Vietnam: Education: BA degree, Faculty of Laws, Saigon; Master degree in Business Administration, USA; Graduated from The Infantry School Thu Duc and Defense Graduate School with highest honor; Former Colonel in the ARVN; Chief of Staff, 2nd Army Corp, Pleiku, Central Vietnam; Write verses at school age. Have part in CHTY (Flowers of Love) Vol.3-97, Vol.4-98. Reside in Orange County, California

TINA THANH HUONG

Born in Hue, Central Vietnam; Education: MS degree in Psychology, University of Illinois 1966; Real Estate Specialist in Sacramento, California.

NAM GIAO

Born in Tây Ninh, South Vietnam; Former officer of the ARVN, former teacher; have poems published in newspapers and magazines in Saigon before 1975. Publication: Tuổi Rừng(Jungle Age 1973), Như Bóng Mây Tan (Like the Fading Clouds 1974) Chuyện Chúng Mình (Our Story 1975) Vùng Ký Ức (Remembrance with Phạm Ngọc 1997). Have part in CHTY (Flowers of Love) Vol.2-96, Vol.3-97, Vol.4-98. Member of the Vietnamese Amateur Poets Society. Reside in Glendale, Arizona.

HUYNH NGOC DIEP

A self-taught painter, who owned his own art studio in Vietnam before 1975, founder of Skyline Graphics in California; his oil paintings have been exhibited in Northern California, the water color painting on this cover is from his fall collections. Reside in Cupertino, California

NGUYEN THI KHANH MINH
Poet - Saigon, Vietnam

NGUYEN DUC CUONG

Born in Saigon, South Vietnam; former officer of the ARVN; Write music since 1989; He have collaborated with Quốc Dũng (a well known musician in Vietnam) in writing many of the popular love songs, they have also produced a music video entitle "Tình Yêu và Nỗi Nhớ" (Love and Remembrance) in 1996; Have part in CHTY (Flowers of Love) Vol.3-97, Vol-4-98. Publication: finished three collection of poems: Ta Xa Nhau Thành Thơ, Thiên Nhiên, Chân Dung. Have published "Nơi Tình Yêu Ẩn Náu" (The Place Where The Love's Hiding - with three other poets -1998)

NGUYEN THUY LINH

Pen name Băng Châu, Thuỳ Linh Thường Vũ; born in North Vietnam; Publication: Poetic works: Tuổi Đôi Mươi, Mùa Xuân Không Nắng, Màu Nhớ Penseé, Biển Sao Đêm, Biển Mây Tên Em và Cuộc Đời. Several Poems set to music: Đỉnh Sường Mù, Vùng Lá Me Bay. Reside in Tacoma, Washington.

NGUYEN VAN CUONG

Real name Nguyễn Thương Quê; born in Mỹ Thạnh, Cam Ranh Province, Central Vietnam; Former official of the Vietnamese Government before 1975; member of the Vietnamese Reporter Union; International Pen, Vietnamese Amateur Poets Society. First Prize, Literature Contest by Tiền Phong Quân Đội Magazine, 1971. Contributing writer for Lang Van, The Ky 21 and many other magazines; Have part in CHTY *(Flowers of Love) Vol2-96, Vol.3-97, Vol.4-98. Reside in Bergen, Norway.*

DIEM THY

Born in Thủ Đức, South Vietnam; Former student of Marie Curie High; BA degree form Faculty of Letters and Vạn Hạnh Han University; Former official of the Ministry of Economy; write verses at school age; Secretary General of Chân Trời Mới Magazine (Paris); Since 1993 President of ASOTA, Paris; Editor in Chief of Periodical Ngày Mới - Paris; Reside in Paris, France.

THANH THANH

THANH THANH is Nhuận Xuân Lê's pen name. He leads the "Construction" poetry and prose group depicted as one of the main branches of the Vietnamese Cultural Secular Tree whose diagram was exhibited at the unique pre-1975 National Cultural Festival in Saigon, capital of the former Republic of Vietnam. He is a lifetime member of the International Society of Poets, a member of the Academy of American Poets, etc. Author of "Về Vùng Chiến Thuật" (Back to the front lines, memoirs), The untold causes of the US-backed South Vietnam's fall, he has just published "Cơn Ác Mộng" (The Nighmare, poems).

- CONTENT -

- CONTENT -

- CONTENT -

Flowers of Love • Poems collection • Cover design Huynh Ngoc Diep • Art direction Ha Anh Tu • Typesetting Nguyen Ham • Presented by The Vietnamese Amateur Poets Society • VSAP P.O Box 246958 Sacramento, Ca 95824 USA • *tel 916.391.5277 • fax 916.736.0608* *•email: haanhtu@worldnet.att.net*